WHAT STILL YIELDS
JAKKY BANKONG-OBI

For Max Dotuchowo Ochagu, who is always my light and wonder

* * *

This is a work of fiction. All names, characters, places, and incidents are a product of the author's imagination. Any resemblance to real events or persons, living or dead, is entirely coincidental.

Published by Akashic Books
©2023 Jakky Bankong-Obi

ISBN: 978-1-63614-129-9

All rights reserved
Printed in China
First printing

Akashic Books
Brooklyn, New York
Instagram, Twitter, Facebook: AkashicBooks
E-mail: info@akashicbooks.com
Website: www.akashicbooks.com

African Poetry Book Fund
Prairie Schooner
University of Nebraska
110 Andrews Hall
Lincoln, Nebraska 68588

TABLE OF CONTENTS

Preface by Mahtem Shiferraw 5

In a Year of Flowers 7
Bougainvillea 9
Say 10
Reincarnation as the Flowers on Your Sisters' Grave 11
Brazen 12
Epiphany 13
The Bare Facts of Our Divergences 14
In the Light of Wonder 15
Ideograms for the Hawk-moth and for the Aftermath Fire 16
Color Bird: Cento 17
False Leads 19
Two Things 21

Notes 22
Acknowledgments 23

PREFACE
by Mahtem Shiferraw

In Jakky Bankong-Obi's chapbook, *What Still Yields*, there is a field, both imagined and real, filled with flowers; in it, aloes, wild Clerondendrum, and ixora make an appearance; as do bougainvillea, Jatropha, and frangipanis, a new blooming set on a land that seems to be in waiting, always in waiting. This blooming, this beauty, is fleeting; a temporary mercy the flowers must inhabit in order to hunker down and survive, in order to root again. There is something sacred here, yielding throughout this emerging Nigerian poet's collection, something left unsaid; something tender and torn, a rebirth that seems so ordinary.

Yet the speaker in this collection is keenly observant; at times a witness, at times complicit in her own truth-telling, she occupies the space between the rooting and the blooming, a space both sacred and filled with aching. There is instruction to make a new fire upon yesterday's white ash; a sister gone too soon is reincarnated as flowers; and lives are held through the beauty of shared memories. What yields, perhaps, is something unnamed; a thing being unearthed slowly throughout the collection, an unrooting of sorts that is done intentionally by Bankong-Obi's speaker, extracted bit by bit through each poem.

Between the language of rooting, and the silences that are placed at critical points throughout the collection, we get a sense of what moves the poet beyond herself. In the poem "The Bare Facts of Our Divergences," Bankong-Obi writes, "They say there are no maps for how migratory birds fly. / It's all instinct, wholly primal—something like desire— / the astonishment of it." This same instinct is the one that drives the speaker to observe her world in such a poignant and nuanced way, as if she's feeling the call of it, pulled by the same astonishment that maps the skies to migratory birds. And, like the birds, the speaker has taken the freedom to be enthralled in such beauty without necessarily being tied to her uprooting. In fact, even more adamant "sometimes we make new light / just for / pounding rain over bruises, pulsing" ("Color Bird: Cento"). Light and loss walk along the same lines, not against each other, but rather, part of the same being, part of the same story of bruising. It's as if the speaker has reached a seeing where the clarity is both new and ancient, where loss is not just made of aching and death, but where it also yields something filled with beauty, perhaps even something filled with light.

However, in reiterating this subtly throughout the collection, Bankong-Obi is hardly sentimental about it, nor can one sense an innocuous desperation that attempts to mask the loss and aching with beauty and light. Rather, there is a knowing to Bankong-Obi's speakers; each one has gone through a loss that has moved them, transformed them, rearranged them, and by extension, we undergo through the same metamorphoses as well. Told to "Look at it this way: / the point isn't just about how hard it is to face the cruelty of loss / but to stay soft, to grow new wings" ("False Leads"), we understand that this knowing stems from a tenderness that has been earned, a softness that originated because the speaker has undergone through such insurmountable loss, that there is nothing left to do but stay in a state of constant tenderness.

This is what moves us: the earnestness, the truth-telling stripped of all of its adorning metaphors or images, simply the body, the loss, the beauty, all of it coexisting all at once, like water entering air, like a body remembering the hunger it needs—without both, there is no rooting to be done. So perhaps, what still yields, throughout the collection and beyond, is the edifice of beauty the poet has built for us, bit by bit, a safe refuge for us to inhabit in our particulars and unprepossessing ways.

Bankong-Obi is a poet that haunts us with her knowing, the dexterity of her speakers moving in space and time, and most of all, she is a storyteller of deep thought, and much needed tenderness. Here is where you come to rest, where your rooting can take place without being unearthed.

IN A YEAR OF FLOWERS

In a year of flowers I confess, I cannot tell Cirsium
from gardenias in December's austere mien.
Tropical and perennial, their scurried stalks
remind me: *despite air, the fallow field.*
                    The mud-caked river. Long and drawn out
                    winter of snowed in meadows elsewhere.

Still.
Praise the resilience of aloes, wild
Clerodendrum and the Ixora's dendritic limbs
fingering the crusted and bare spine, pistillate
through harmattan's dolorous days. Wait
                  until February thaws
                  grim-eyed nettles, rangy

Jatropha and a scattering clematis from the waking
gyre; the world, a slow moving garden-reveal
April sings in the muted tones of frangipanis & morning
glories. All of it dewy with the sheen of first love.
                That bated breath.
                Hum before the kiss—is May,

a culled storm that breaks into June just right, it sets
everything blooming. Lush and carpeting green moss
in cool meadows I could laze forever in
but the jacarandas' bunting. W*hat will be will be* love's
                  sweet blush hectic as
                  a flush of hydrangeas in July,

roses and calla lilies rouging in their sultry mead: the humidity,
a fecund domain. What riot of moths and bees
will resist. To *nectar?* The honey and the honeycomb.
                      The fore-glow of August
                            as the quiet reckoning of linear time.

The harvest is a bouquet of posies, accents
of celosia and jasmine, lantana and queen-of-the-night.
Tendrils of trade winds on the heels of a crisp October
rumors of distant storms we have weathered.
                          A climatic anticlimax we can tell
                            this time will be harder. To survive,

they will have to go back, hunker down
to seed. To bloom again,
root.

BOUGAINVILLEA

My fingertips, scented
and nectar sweetened, feted in
dry season blossoms, tender
and spike shorn; split raw with familiar ache;
bougainvillea-ed. The blooms, bold and vining
petals skyward pointing, as if praying or votive,
the way humans yearn for beauty, avid
and ravenous like a candle lit and flickering
races to burn itself out. Eager, I pluck at them
and leave bits of myself, human sacrifice
for the perennial altar. Because beauty rarely
leaves you unscathed. When she touches you,
she splits you open, tender soft like new birth.
A sacred thing.

SAY

Say you want more.
Say your want is an ocean, vast and turbulent, swallowing
everything alive into itself. Because you are your mother's daughter
and you have never had enough of anything.

Say you yearn.
Say you yearn to know how to love a man and to get
him to love you too. Because you are your father's daughter
and when he died, he left you a legacy of ignorance.

Say you question.
Say you question why this sun of fire never embraces
the moon of dreams. Because fear is an old grave that often swallows
newborn things and a caterpillar must learn to eat her safe place to wings

Say you are woman.
And fate is what remains after the day is exhausted
as the night always clean-slates into another day to begin again.
And your heart sings its truest song when it sings of itself.

REINCARNATION AS THE FLOWERS ON YOUR SISTERS' GRAVE
for Adinne

                      And maybe this is how you came to be the last.
                      Daughter, a child to be loved after a lifetime
                      of trying to keep alive. In another native tongue,
                      you are *ogbanje*, in another time when
                      your mother believed in soul mates. Said
                      "the gods gave us this men and their wrath."

But when you wilted again and again,
she tried to suckle you on the lees of your dead matter.
Fed you your gnarled navel for seven days
until your tongue mustered—
like fungus fingers inside a carcass
lapping on old bone, ore smelting in the barrow

                      of mouth. Until you maggoted your way through
                      dead tissue through the lost dreams of a once wanted
                      life. Until you exhausted the peril of your past
                      into flowers, incarnated at last.

BRAZEN
for my grandmother

Herbs cooked in blackened pot, in water adding nothing, over open flame invoke the mother, the father, all the ancestors near and far. Dig earth, plant things; pull roots, chop at stems, deep cuts, swift and beautiful snips, light handed razor-sharp kisses of pain. Make place for new growth. Intrude, pour salt on fresh wound; kill the tender thing while it is still new, give no room for the old malice to creep in. A poultice for festering sores, draw out poison from the hidden crevices, entice the harm out of limbs of comfort. *Ori* and palm kernel oil spell the air, stand in moonshadow, give in to yearning, cross times three, make wishes, pour water from the calabash, make a libation, spittle to navel, your girl child comes, bearing your mother again. In the hot afternoon sun, cut two marks on the baby soft skin, mar and blemish, dark ash from night lamp, rub in, ward off infant death. With pestle and stone, feed. The lemon grass and stalk, slender the reeds, garland the dance, wave the heels, palm wine and kola nut, rhythm and woo, see through the sweet, the tangy, pine and sing, impudent green till tawny, till old and worn. Make fire on yesterday's white ash, cogent a far conquest, bridge to the root, maze wonder. Make more, take life, barefoot and brazen. Brazen. Brazen.

EPIPHANY

Sometimes on the cusp
of a tropical storm, as the sun
floats to shelter, stealing
from cloud to cloud, she
finds a slit in space, drips
tints of golden light and
spotlights on the shape of
things, highlights; slant of line,
curve in form. Suddenly,
the unveiling of a new vista,
in old and familiar places.
Say epiphany.

THE BARE FACTS OF OUR DIVERGENCES

They say there are no maps for how migratory birds fly.
It's all instinct, wholly primal—something like desire—
the astonishment of it.

A call in the blood for the object of one's deepest longing
that sets a heart ribbing out of its cage toward
a horizon that is ultimately disappearing.

If I were to die anywhere on this skein and grain
my mother's womb is as good a place to root and bud.
Blessed be my earthing in the rain forest and umber.

But I am made of forgotten gods and the dispersal
of Neem leaves in duress of harmattan winds, so,
I libate to the deep loving of woman in the medusa

because in all her wildest fury and delirium,
against an insatiate world, love is still the strongest
of shields for all that is my tender and veiled spine.

And in this age-old coming and going where the sun is to skin what the sea is to fish; I say drown me in the depths of this ocean, and tide me in the bare facts of all her divergences.

IN THE LIGHT OF WONDER
for Dotuchowo

Side by side. We watch an orange sun defunct the sky & the half-moon shimmer of mid-August unveil   the gloaming.   How the future abuts the past & all present exigencies fade.   & memory becomes all but night's inky overcast—where only the brightest fragments shine—like stars punctuating the dark. I know this moment will be ours forever.   *The beauty of shared memories is that they hold us together.*
Mother to son,   we bait the telescope   pending the stars' stellar preen. Your hand in mine,   a weight   I will carry forever   & pray this light never quits your eyes   & the worth of all expectations   shine in the luminous aspects of your face, a mirror::a door   I open & suddenly a reachable miracle;   joy.   Your laughter like a shooting star,   unfettered across all our skies.
& it grows & grows   so it seems the night's prized constellations, which were at first impossible   & removed now spotlight   here.   As though an aperture has somehow unfolded this ordinary life into wonder.

IDEOGRAMS FOR THE HAWK-MOTH AND FOR THE AFTERMATH FIRE

I. Dusk is something to wallow in.
II. Antlers on a hilltop, sunned and bifurcating.
III. Scry of crow on the withering branch.
IV. Black shadows feathering secret rendezvous with home.
V. The gloaming, a masque headdress: relic of a time honored ritual of uncovering.
VI. Audience of crickets in the underbrush,
VII. *whatever sees us, sees us.*
VIII. Deep ancestral hour of night.
XIV. A felled log
X. brush of mushroom beside
XI. longing unmakes.
XII. Haunt of charcoal on ochre skin
XIII. dancing under the full moon,
XIV. lightning strikes three times,
XV. a thousand fires kindle and rage.
XVI. Lovers learn the shape of desire.
XVII. Secret: body crumbles at the slightest touch.
XVIII. A moth's chitinous wing
XIX. arcs you into open flame.
XX. Blurring the lines of luminance and shatter.

COLOR BIRD: CENTO
for the malimbé. for the long impossible flight home.

Love, let me begin by saying that yes I am afraid of dying.
So when I say I want to fling myself into the sun, I mean,

You do not get used to being left behind.
Every loss is a reminder of the previous.

I have listened to the beat
of slow wings across the sky.

Black shadows fall
against the southern sky;

the occasion / infant light / maybe burning / light needing to be.
weary from its travels / sometimes we make new light / just for

pounding rain over bruises, pulsing.
Now a field of heartbeats. Open.

All of my bones /
light enough / to bury.

Perhaps the nuances are intentional.
Men want to see you bleed my mother says

of every dream, your father is where the act
of missing something first took root.

Geometry has put our home at the center of the world: grief's capital & suddenly
all the flowers are sick, we are not sure who to save.

Sealed with bruises. I am running back & forth between the house of silence &
 the house
this heat wave, mother of our circling, the name we gave to the far side of the
 horizon—

Water quenching our ruined kingdom of wilderness
air suspended into nooses. A brackish aftertaste.

I understand it is impossible to love a thing without making
it yours. Each scar, a color bird, is my love's signature.

FALSE LEADS
for G, after reading Breai Mason-Campbell and Nâzim Hikmet.

In the receding light of the day
my eyes are thirsty, the world is fine.

You could never get enough of grassy meadows,
ribbons of green and lemon, fronding & cheerful.

I am at the doorway of the police station
a slow wind rustles through the field of lemongrass.

And beyond, there are birds singing the evening
I want to believe I can hear your voice in the fray.

Inside, someone undone by grief crows brokenly
"All this grieving and the dead stay dead."

It's true, we are born with the same assurance of death,
meaning we do not always have to go looking for some things to find us.

The city is known for its throng of mourning doves,
to leave the roost is to know the way back.

But the real injury is a stray bullet, the indifference of its plunder
—a raptor's swoop and stolid violence.

A gun shot inside a dove's nest would hardly miss,
by which I mean deplume its flight.

I could never look into the faces of the dead
on the TV screens, the bodies pile and pile.

Look at it this way:
the point isn't just about how hard it is to face the cruelty of loss
but to stay soft, to grow new wings.

TWO THINGS

Press two moist things together
where one shrinks, the other swells

the way water enters and air
escapes, making a body ripen

and cells remembering hunger
the mouth eats, in osmosis for growth.

The way rain forest foragers
unearth archaeal lushness in dry season

and undersoil water to heartwood
seduce sweetness from a core of rotting things.

And how where the sky meets the sea,
a new horizon opens at the edge of seeing.

NOTES

"Color Bird: Cento" includes lines from:

"portrait of a saphhic as a supernova" by Emma Chan (*perhappened mag*)
"Shedding" by Roberta Amanda Yemofio (Contemporary Ghanaian Writers' Series, Issue III: *Equanimity*)
"Migratory Birds" by Dora Sigerson Shorter (All Poetry.com)
Birds of Passage by Henry Wadsworth Longfellow (Dodo Press)
"Litany for Silver Nitrate Saints" by Lee Potts (*Firmament*: Sublunary Editions)
"Instructions for the Moon" from *Deus ex Nigrum* by Jasmine Reid (Honeysuckle Press)
"Debole" by Devanshi Khetarpal (*Redivider Journal*)
"New Organism [I want to think like a magi]" by Andrea Rexilius (Poets.Org)
"Homeward" from *Hinge* by Alycia Pirmohamed (Ignition Press)
"Banach-Tarski/Suddenly" by Akpa Arinzechukwu (*20.35 Africa: An Anthology of Contemporary Poetry Vol. III*)
"2015 Paris Agreement" by Ojo Taiye (*trampset*)
"Fifteen Ways of Saying Hunger" from *Ghost Tracks* by Sneha Subramanian Kanta (Louisiana Literature)
"Of My Love's Signature" by Ernest Ogunyemi (*Ermite Poetry*)

ACKNOWLEDGMENTS

The following poems were first published in the following journals/anthologies, with thanks to the editors:

"The Bare Facts of Our Divergences"—*Reliquiae Journal*
"Say" and "Bougainvillea"—*Memento: An Anthology of Contemporary Nigerian Poetry*
"Two Things"—*Amberflora*
"False Leads"-*Pipewrench Magazine*
"In the Light of Wonder"—*Capsule Stories*
"Brazen"—*Zarf Poetry*
"In a Year of Flowers" and "Ideograms for the Hawk-moth and for the Aftermath Fire"—*Poetry Review*